Three Days That Shook Edinburgh

by

HARRY McSHANE

AK PRESS

Edinburgh   London   San Francisco

British Library Cataloguing in Publication Data

McShane, Harry
  Three Days That Shook Edinburgh:
  Story of the Historic Scottish Hunger March.
  New ed
  I. Title
  322.209411

  ISBN 1-873176-77-5

New Edition 1994 by
  AK Press
  22 Lutton Place
  Edinburgh
  EH8 9PE

Typeset and design by Steven D. Reid.

Contents

Introduction

The reprint of this pamphlet, originally published in 1933 by the National Unemployed Workers Movement (NUWM)* will be of interest to working class people in Scotland and the world over. Although it relates to events over sixty years ago, topicality and relevance are not lost with the passing of time. Massive numbers of people were out of work in those days, with the attendant poverty and misery, and a government imposed "means test" that was universally hated. Today the situation is much worse, with one in ten of the Scottish workforce on the dole - or to put it another way - over a quarter of a million people unemployed in Scotland, and over three million in the UK without jobs, even though the present Tory government has massaged the figures regularly to take at least another million off the total.

Readers of *Three Days That Shook Edinburgh* will themselves feel angry that so little has been done by the labour movement to organise and fight back against the ravages of unemployment in the present situation. When the present recession was looming large, the Labour Party and the trade unions set up an impressive demonstration in Glasgow, with fifty thousand people taking part. This show of strength turned out to be a flash in the pan, amounting to no more than the letting off of steam, powered by a cascade of rhetoric. Subsequent protest marches were grandly described as "Peoples Marches For Jobs", but they were only fringe events. The daily growing number of unemployed were not involved in organising them to any great degree, and compared to the efforts, the imagination and the organisation of the NUWM in the thirties they were puny affairs.

In a situation where more than ten people are chasing every vacancy; where more than a million workers have been unemployed for more than a year; when the majority of school leavers can't find a job, and in many cases are not entitled to any benefits; and finally, when most men and women over fifty can be taken off the unemployment register to reduce the total, and they realise that they may never work again - has the time not come when we must raise the fundamental question of the very existence of the capitalist system?

---

*National Unemployed Workers Movement - formed in 1921 by delegates from local unemployed committees. Though its leading activists were mainly Communists like Harry McShane and Wal Hannington, the NUWM maintained its independence from the Communist Party. The Labour Party and the Trade Union leaderships opposed any moves by the unemployed to organise themselves and consistently refused to cooperate with the NUWM.

Long before labour leaders became respectable, they discussed and organised on street corners and, as this pamphlet shows, fought for decent living conditions in the midst of mass unemployment. Is it not about time that unemployed workers centres were used as centres of agitation and struggle instead of bingo and pool?

The pioneers of the working class unions did have a dream - it was called Socialism. In a world where what is on offer is only booms and slumps with the occasional war thrown in, there must be a better way.

When, in February 1993, Major came to a £100 a head fund-raising dinner for the Tory Party in Scotland, he was confronted by shop stewards from Rosyth dockyard concerned about their jobs, due to the threat of closure. Of course, they were wasting their time. They had protested; organised petitions; lobbied Parliament on many occasions; badgered Lang, the Scottish Secretary and Rifkind, the Defence Secretary, but they had forgotten to get in touch with the invisible man - God! The Reverend William Morris, head man at the Glasgow Cathedral, did not forget. Sitting at the top table, he led the diners in the saying of grace. One newspaper did report that the audience seemed rather stunned as the worthy Reverend prayed for the Lord to intervene in favour of Rosyth. Indeed, he went much further than that, beseeching God to guide the self-righteous John Major, so that he would award the new Trident contract to Fife. Incredible isn't it? So that's about all this motley crew can do for the employed or the unemployed. The truth is, only the workers can help themselves.

In 1983, when he was ninety years old, Harry McShane was interviewed by the magazine *Socialist Review*, and had this to say:

"Last night on television Michael Foot was talking about unemployment, that it would be with us for a long time to come. For the first time he was admitting that unemployment is a permanent feature under capitalism. He had no solution to offer, and he said "we can't raise people's hopes". We have to make propaganda and say clearly there can be no solution to the problem of unemployment under capitalism. We have to argue that alongside the fight to improve the conditions of the unemployed we must fight all the time to change the system. That is the only solution..."

Les Foster

The original publication included four photographs. Unfortunately the publishers could only locate one print which could be reproduced.

Foreword

The Hunger March of June 1933 was an event of outstanding importance.

We who had the honour and privilege of taking part in the actual leadership of the March can testify to the courage, the amazing self-discipline, the capacity for self-sacrifice, and the unfailing and unflagging spirit of the Marchers themselves. These Marchers acted throughout in the true sense of being delegates of the great mass of workers, employed and unemployed, throughout Scotland, and the Scottish Working Class may well be proud not only of the achievements of the March, but of the Marchers themselves.

We were impressed, above all, by the tremendous enthusiasm and support manifested towards the march by the Scottish Working Class. Everywhere we went, the Workers and Marchers fused in one mighty army. All the petty barriers which the Tory Councillors, the Capitalist Press, Police (aided by their eternal discredit by the Labour and Trade Union leaders) tried to erect, were shattered to fragments on the great onrush of Working Class solidarity. The class character of the March swept everything else aside as superfluous and triumphed clear and unmistakable. But for this solidarity the March could not have done what it did, achieved the successes it did achieve.

This March, one of the very first fruits of the drive and urge for Working Class Unity, was a signal and historic triumph for the United Front.* Here, before the eyes of all, striding triumphant over all the narrow, petty quibbles of Reformist leaders, was the living United Front in action.

Of the achievements of this March, these are told in detail in the pamphlet. We wish only to make one observation upon them. These achievements illustrate what can be done provided the masses of the working men and women are thoroughly aroused and the case is explained clearly to them.

---

*The United Front was the Communist Party's policy at that time. It called for a united front of the Communist Party, the Labour Party, the unions and other working class organisations in the struggle against Fascism. McShane was sceptical of this policy and he contrasted the "living United Front" of employed and unemployed.

These achievements are an inspiration and an incentive to every honest and sincere worker in Scotland. They have lifted our whole movement up; given courage to the faint-hearted; inspired hope in the seemingly hopeless and despondent; heartened and lifted up the laggards.

The organisation of this March was marvellously perfect, a tribute to the NUWM, the organiser of the March. Everywhere the cooking and feeding arrangements went like clockwork, eloquent testimony to the magnificent organising abilities latent in the proletariat.

We hope that tens and thousands of Scottish workers will read and study this short pamphlet. They will find a message here which will show them that there is a way to defeat our enemies, to beat back attacks on our already too miserable standards and to win fresh demands and concessions. They will see that there is no need for pessimism, that faith in the masses, faith in ourselves, faith in our cause expressed in the Revolutionary United Front will achieve victory.

The Red thread running through this pamphlet is the Triumph of Mass Action, Mass Pressure. Let us all take this message to heart: carry the fight into every county, town, village, hamlet, into every street and tenement, into every TU Branch and Co-operative.

Inspired by the glorious Hunger March to Edinburgh, we will fight and win the vitally necessary demands of the Unemployed and Employed Workers of Scotland.

JOHN McGOVERN, MP
Independent Labour Party*

AITKEN FERGUSON
Communist Party

---

*The Independent Labour Party (ILP) - formed in 1893, it became one of the organisations that set up and became part of the Labour Party.

8

Story of the

Historic Scottish Hunger March

by

HARRY McSHANE

On Friday, 9th June 1933, along the main roads leading to Edinburgh, columns of men were marching; men with bands, banners, slogans,everyone equipped with knapsack and blanket, their field cookers on ahead: an army in miniature, an unemployed army, the Hunger Marchers.

In the ranks were men of all political opinions - Labour men, Communists, ILP; there were Trade Unionists and non-Unionists; there were even sections of women marchers - all marching four abreast, shoulder to shoulder, keeping step, surging along rhythmically.

Here was the United Front of the workers, one of the first fronts of the drive for Unity now being made in all parts of Britain.

YOUTH

An outstanding feature of the March was the predominant part played in it by the young workers. At least 50 per cent of the Marchers could be classified as young workers. Their discipline, courage and determination were of the very highest order and showed how the Youth can assist to a tremendous degree the fight of the Unemployed.

This March, with its strong Youth representation, is a living refutation of the pessimists who assert that the young workers are not interested in the struggle. It drives home the necessity of the most careful and extensive preparations being made so that in every area and locality the young workers will be drawn into the general mass activity. It reinforces a thousand times the urgent necessity of building strong Youth sections of the Unemployed Movement.

WHY THEY MARCHED

The marchers were going to Edinburgh, endeavouring to secure an interview with Sir G Collins, Secretary of State for Scotland. They proposed to lay before him the steadily worsening conditions of the unemployed masses of Scotland, to demand increased relief for semi-starving men, women and children, and to put certain carefully thought out proposals for work schemes which would help to give employment to tens of thousands of the unemployed army; to demand the ending of the embargo on Russian goods which was preventing employment for 60,000 Engineering workers (including many in Scotland) because of stoppage of Soviet orders. They marched for work, for bread, and for maintenance of all unemployed.

The marching unemployed were the delegates, the representatives of their four hundred thousand unemployed comrades at home. Every trade, every industry, was present. The workers of Scotland stood behind the Marchers, stood behind their demands for work and maintenance, stood behind their Hunger Trek to Edinburgh.

OUR DEMANDS

(1) Abolition of the Means Test.
(2) That children of unemployed be granted 1s 6d per week extra, and that adult unemployed and adult dependants be granted 3s per week extra. These increases to apply to all unemployed whether in receipt of statutory or transitional payments or in receipt of Public Assistance.
(3) That rents be reduced 25 per cent.
(4) That the Social Service Schemes and all voluntary labour connected with the same be repudiated. In addition, the lifting of the Embargo on the Soviet Union and conclusion of a new Trade Agreement.

The Hunger March of June 1933, was a coping stone to a whole series of mass activities which had swept Scotland. In Glasgow, in Renfrewshire, in Fifeshire, Lanarkshire, Dumbartonshire, even in far north Aberdeen and Fraserburgh, the mass movement of the unemployed had developed. Despite sneers, insults, batonings, jailings, the agitation had developed, thousands of meetings held, incessant delegations and deputising, huge popular petitions containing the demands of the unemployed organised, mass demonstrations held. Clashes with the police were frequent (in Glasgow, due to plain clothes policemen provocation, a fierce fight took place on Glasgow Green and fourteen policemen were injured). A tremendous petition, containing the signatures of over 112,000 people was organised, a concession of 1s 6d per child literally torn out of the Glasgow PAC* by mass pressure - only to have the National Government† step in, in order to prevent a workers' victory in Glasgow.

In Fife, in Dumbartonshire, even in Ayrshire, the workers forced concessions.

County Hunger Marches in Fife, Ayrshire, Lanarkshire, were organised. They were very successful. More and more workers were being brought into the struggle; hope was being given to the faint-hearted and the lukewarm. The struggle against the means Test, the Dole Cuts, the Anomalies Act was intensifying. The stage was set for an all-Scottish Hunger March to raise the fight to a still greater height. The famous Hunger March in June was the result.

Not an isolated event, not a stunt, but the logical development, the coping stone, of the mass local activities throughout the winter and spring.

The preparations for the March were more thorough and wide-spread than anything hitherto. Not simply to organise contingents of marchers, but to organise a mass working-class support for the March contingents, to bring factory workers, Trade Union branches, Co-operatives, Trades Councils into the March, to get active support in popularising the Demands.

Hunger Marchers' Councils were organised in the areas composed of delegates from as many working-class organisations as possible; hundreds of March Recruiting Meetings were held; Trade Union Branches circularised, and in some cases visited; public correspondence initiated with Sir Godfrey Collins and with Town Councils and Trades Councils on the main routes to Edinburgh; resolutions passed from a very large number of Trade Union branches and from meetings, demanding that Collins be present; Town Councils and Councillors deputised; a regular series of propagandist and agitational activities which had a tremendous result in focusing attention on the March and in breaking down the former isolation of the unemployed from the employed and trade union workers.

All this time the recruiting for the March contingents was going on, the Field Kitchens were prepared, money and foodstuffs collected - a significant feature, indicating the progress made in breaking down

---

*Public Assistance Committee - PAC's were appointed by local authorities to administer the granting of relief for the unemployed.

†In 1931, unable to deal with the economic crisis Ramsey MacDonald, the then Labour Prime Minister, dissolved the Labour Government and formed a coalition government with the Tories and Liberals - the National Government.

isolation, was the very fine response from Trade Union branches and Co-operatives in sending donations and passing resolutions demanding that Collins come to Edinburgh. The Recruiting Form, as follows, enabled the best type of Marchers to be recruited, and prevented our enemies saying that anyone was mislead.

SCOTTISH HUNGER MARCH
Declaration Form

May, 1933.

I..*Name*

....*Address*

promise that while on the March I will observe strict discipline, as I realise that unless discipline is observed the greatest dangers will arise for the marchers.

I also undertake to stay in Edinburgh until the main body of marchers leave. I have been informed that there are no guarantees about returning on any particular day. I come on the march with that understanding, and will observe the agreement.

I understand the significance of this march and fully support the demands to the Government.

Signed...

NOTE - No one can be allowed on the march who has not filled in this form.

THE CONCENTRATION AGAINST THE MARCH

Never at any time has there been such concentration against any March as against this. Capitalist Town councils, Labour leaders, Trades Union bureaucrats, with the Press, Police and Sir Godfrey Collins joining in, all united in an unholy alliance denouncing the March, refusing any assistance, trying to intimidate the workers with their refusal to grant either recognition, food or accommodation. All along the routes, at the suggested stopping places - Kilsyth, Bo'ness, Airdrie, etc - there was an obstinate refusal to grant accommodation for the Marchers, a concentrated campaign of opposition and vilification on the part of the capitalists, the Labour and Trade Union leaders.

The situation was sharpening, the sides were becoming clearer defined. On the one hand the Unemployed Workers united with the Trade Union branches and Co-operative Guilds and factory workers organising the March; on the other the capitalist Press and Police, plus the capitalist councillors and Labour and Trade Union leaders mobilising and uniting to prevent and destroy the March.

THE MARCH BEGINS

Word came through on 6th June that Aberdeen and Dundee contingents had set out to link up with Fife in Kirkcaldy. The March was on! The Ayrshire contingent linked up with Lanarkshire and marched via Shotts and East Calder.

Renfrewshire and Dumbartonshire came to Glasgow and set out via Coatbridge, Airdrie, Bathgate, and Broxburn; with them marched a women's section.

The Glasgow men set out via Kilsyth and Falkirk, where they were joined by Stirlingshire, on to Bo'ness and Corstorphine.

By Friday afternoon all the contingents were under way. Along the four main highroads to Edinburgh tramped steadily the Hunger Marchers, bands playing, flags flying, cheery and determined. Not a single contingent had accommodation guaranteed, not a single contingent entertained the slightest doubt that it would be secured. They knew that the pressure of the masses was something that no Town Council nor bureaucratic Provost could long stand against.

In Glasgow there was a tremendous send-off; thousands of people gathered at George Square; and as the March started - headed by Comrades McGovern; Heenan of the ILP; Aitken Ferguson, Communist Party; Henderson, Glasgow Organiser of the NUWM; and Harry McShane, Scottish Organiser of the NUWM and the March - there was a great send-off. All the road out to Bishopbriggs a huge demonstration accompanied the Marchers, then lined the roadside, and cheered the March contingent as it set off on its first lap (Kilsyth).

THE FIRST BARRIER SURMOUNTED

In this town the Provost and the Labour Town Council had refused any assistance whatever. "No use the Marchers coming here"; Nothing could be done"; "Nobody wanted them"; etc. But what a reception at Kilsyth! The entire town, almost without exception, turned out to greet the Marchers. the Town Council meeting scheduled for that night was hastily abandoned, and the Councillors and Provost disappeared. Quarters were found for the men in the Salvation Army headquarters; a gigantic meeting was held in the Park by comrades McGovern, Heenan, McShane, Ferguson; a unanimous vote of support for the Marchers was given.

The townspeople were ours - no doubt, hesitation or dubiety about where they stood in relation to the March. They, like the overwhelming mass of the workers everywhere the March touched, solidly supported the Hunger Marchers.

This story of Kilsyth is the experience of every contingent - barriers erected by the enemies, crumbling before the surge of working-class mass pressure aroused by the very appearance of the Marchers.

All along the route, in every town and village, in almost every cottage the workers came out to welcome the marching unemployed. Coppers, which could ill be spared, clinked into the boxes; women with tears in their eyes, wishing the men "good luck" and dropping their contributions into the collecting tins.

No hair-splitting arguments among the masses, no asking themselves whether the Right Honourable Geo. Lansbury MP* had given the March his pontifical blessing or not, no question as to whether Mr Citrine† or the TUC endorsed or did not endorse the March.

No! The workers realised instinctively that this was their own people who were marching, their own class, kith and kin; it was "their side", and anybody who opposed it was on the other side.

The class character of the March broke through all the flimsy arguments of the Labour and Trade Union leaders and showed, as in a lightening flash, where they stood - on the other side of the barricade.

In this pamphlet there is not one-tenth of the space required to tell of one-half of the episodes of this memorable March, of the heroism and determination that kept men plugging on with feet torn, blistered, bloody, even when their comrades and leaders wanted them to take a bus into Corstorphine; of comrade Heenan, whose feet were in a terrible condition and who wrenched his ankle six miles from Corstorphine, but who obstinately refused even to consider giving up, and kept tramping doggedly on. How can one tell of the humour, the healthy, salty humour,

----

*Leader of the Labour Party
†TUC General Secretary

that refused even to consider downheartedness even when tramping along at the end of a twenty-mile march through two hours of pelting rain? How can one write of the discipline, the comradeship, the glowing loyalty of the marchers, that would have inspired a dead man!

INTO EDINBURGH

At 4pm, Sunday, 11th June, all the contingents reached the Central Meeting Place at Corstorphine. What a sight it was as each contingent marched in; what a cheer they got from the rest!

An especial welcome was given to the women marchers, whose spirit and determination were marvellous.

The staff work at Corstorphine was splendid. Everything worked on ball bearings. The Marchers' own Field Kitchens were in full blast, and in an incredibly short time the whole army was fed.

The whistle goes - Pheep-eep; the contingents form up; then, headed by their bands, off they go into Edinburgh - one thousand strong - in military formation and discipline.

The Edinburgh workers sent out a strong contingent to meet us and march in with us. The streets were lined all the way into Edinburgh with sympathetic workers, tremendous enthusiasm prevailing.

The result was that, seeing what was happening, the Authorities decided on a cautious policy.

We knew beforehand that we could be allowed peacefully to enter Edinburgh. Before the Glasgow contingent left, letters were sent to Sir Godfrey Collins, the Ministry of Labour, the Department of Health and the Education Department, asking them to hear a deputation on Monday 12th June. Three telegrams were received on the road - one from each Department - offering to meet a deputation on Monday at 11am at the Ministry of Labour Office, 44 Drumsheugh Gardens. We had no reply from Sir Godfrey Collins. These telegrams were the first recognition of the March; it was a break through.

THE MARCHERS IN EDINBURGH

The Marchers had now arrived at their destination, despite opposition and rumours to the effect that the March would be called off. We marched to the Mound, where the formation was still maintained. About 20,000 people had assembled here. So dense was the crowd that many could not hear the speeches which were delivered. Councillor Paton gave a speech of welcome, which was replied to by McGovern, Heenan,

Ferguson and McShane. The Marchers then went to the ILP Hall at Bonnington Road, where a meal was provided by the Edinburgh Reception Committee.

The first concession by the Authorities in Edinburgh was when the police agreed to lift the ban on collections in the streets, after the Marchers had declared their intention of collecting from everyone who was prepared to assist the March.

While feeding was going on, a deputation approached the police on the question of accommodation. They came back with a report to the effect that we could have Waverley Market. The deputation had raised the question of blankets or boards being put on the stone floor. This request was refused, and the deputation turned down the offer of the Waverley Market.

The struggle had now begun! The Marchers were lined up and marched off. In reply to enquiries as to where they were going, it was stated that they were going to the police station. The suggestion was then made that we should sleep on Leith Links. We said we would sleep where we could be seen.

When the Marchers reached the Post Office, instead of going to the Police Station, they turned along Princess Street, picked a place past the Mound, took off their kits and sat down! Within a few minutes news came along that McGovern and McShane were wanted by two men in a car. Word was sent back, "We are too tired, let them come here". They came along and told us they had secured the Oddfellows Hall, which we decided to accept.

When, however, the hall was filled up, there was still a considerable number without accommodation. In order to find accommodation the Assistant Chief Constable and Aitken Ferguson went to the Melbourne Hall which is owned by the Scottish Socialist Party. The Assistant Chief Constable appealed for the hall on the grounds of humanity, and offered to pay for it, but was met with a point blank refusal. The Marchers that were left ultimately slept in the police muster rooms. It was two o'clock in the morning before all the Marchers were sheltered.

THE MARCHERS GO TO THE SCOTTISH OFFICE

On Monday after breakfast (which we had at Bonnington Road) we marched to Drumsheugh Gardens where our deputation was to be heard. The Marchers sat outside while the deputation was being heard. The deputation was inside the building for two hours. It was composed of Comrades McGovern, Ross of Lanarkshire, McPherson of Fife, Harley of Greenock, Kelly of the NUR, and McShane. The deputation protested at the absence of Sir Godfrey Collins; and after much discussion, persuaded the officials to telephone through to Collins in London. He persisted in his refusal to meet the Marchers. The deputation expressed its willingness to wait in Edinburgh until he came. In the absence of Collins, the deputation proceeded to put the Marchers' demands before the permanent officials present.

THE DEPUTATION

The deputation demanded the abolition of the Anomalies Act and the Means Test. They stressed the fact that women should not be compelled to go into domestic service, and that there should be an end to voluntary labour under the Social Service Schemes which, they said, was getting people to do work for nothing and the thin end of the wedge for the introduction of compulsory labour in return for Unemployment Benefit. They asked for extensive work schemes such as the construction of the Forth Road bridge and a new arterial road through Glasgow to be put in hand: all work to be paid at trade-union rates of wages and conditions. So far as the Department of Health was concerned, the deputation asked for an extension of benefits under the National Health Insurance scheme, and pressed for the removal of anomalies in the scales of relief paid in various localities. A protest was made against the interference of the Ministry of Health last December when Glasgow Public Assistance Committee recommended an increase for children of unemployed during Christmas and New Year weeks.

In regard to education, the deputation asked for more schools and a supply of better boots and books for the children of the unemployed.

They raised the question of the treatment of the Hamilton "squatters" and stated that they should be properly housed by this time.

They also protested against the embargo on Soviet Russia, which is aggravating the unemployment problem in this country.

The deputation was told that their representations were noted and would be sent to the proper quarter. This was described by the deputation as very unsatisfactory. After further discussion, the deputation rejoined the Marchers outside.

IN PARLIAMENT SQUARE

In the meantime, while we were engaged in these activities, the cooks (in accordance with a pre-arranged plan) had removed the cooking utensils to Parliament Square. Just before two o'clock a large lorry arrived on the scene, laden with camp kitchens, dixies and canteens, large supplies of pies and other foods and trestles and boards.

The three camp-kitchens were soon belching forth large clouds of smoke. Gallons and gallons of tea were made, while boxes containing a large amount of food were unloaded. Some six or eight women assisted the Marchers' own cooks in preparing and serving the food.

The unusual sight in this historical Square attracted large crowds of passers-by, and they seemed inclined to linger to watch the proceedings; but a large body of police arrived on the scene and kept them in motion.

A STRIKING SCENE

"A remarkable scene was presented when the Marchers encamped in the square in orderly lines. Within a few minutes, with packs off, they lined up in long queues at the kitchens and received tea, a sausage roll and two slices of bread, and again settled down in their places to consume their meal. Every corner of the square was utilised, and quite a number of men sat themselves down on the steps at the west door of St. Giles Cathedral, while a score or so others, including a number of women, sat down on the step around the Buccleuch Monument.

After a while, some sought shade in the far corner near the Signet Library. Some, more active, busied themselves in helping with the further distribution of tea, whilst from parts of the encampment came snatches of songs. Large numbers of the public viewed the scene, although they were not encouraged by the police to loiter. In the bright sunshine the Marchers were a colourful gathering, with red flavours very much to the fore, while the owners lay down in ranks, and the appearance of a military bivouac was enhanced when the 'flying squad' of cyclists arrived and 'stacked' machines." - *Edinburgh Press*

After waiting here some time, it was decided that we go to the Meadows where the men could have a rest and hear a report of the deputation.

THEY MARCH THROUGH HOLYROOD

The Marchers' road to the Edinburgh Meadows lay down that historic thorough-fare, the Royal Mile, leading to the historic Royal Palace of Holyrood.*

---

*Being a Glaswegian McShane can be forgiven for confusing Queens Park with The Meadows. Queens Park is the name of the park beside Holyrood Palace, while The Meadows are on Edinburgh's Southside.

Down go the swinging columns, down right to the gates of Holyrood. "Turn to the right", says a police official. The March leaders turn a deaf ear. "Straight On!" "Straight on" it is, right through the Palace grounds itself. The pompous official in charge at the Palace almost took an apoplectic fit! His eyes literally bulged out with mingled astonishment and horror.

In go the columns, a mile of flaming, flaunting scarlet banners, headed by the Maryhill Band playing Connolly's Rebel Song as if their lungs would burst. What a sight!!

The proletariat, the indomitable proletariat in their ragged clothes, have stepped into the most sacred precincts in all Scotland!

The walls and grounds of the Royal Palace of Holyrood - that innermost sanctuary of all the Royal parasites in Scotland's history - echo the tramp of the first legions of the masses. The walls and ground of Holyrood that heard the music of Rizzio, and Mary Queen of Scots, hear the song of that murdered Irish leader, "The Rebel Song", and then the thunderous battle cry of the world's workers, "The Internationale".

Never has Holyrood heard or witnessed anything like this. No wonder the capitalists are shocked to the marrow! Is this a herald of the approaching storm which will shatter their domination for ever? Murdered Connolly lives again; his spirit, his song, his memory inspires these Hunger Marchers as they swing through the grounds and then pass through the other gate.

On to the Meadows, where the men rested, heard a report of the deputation and a statement on the tasks now to be undertaken by Comrades McShane, McGovern and Ferguson.

It is significant that although the Marchers were able to smash the Press boycott on all other activities relating to the March, not a single capitalist Daily mentioned the March through Holyrood. Only the *Daily Worker* reported this event. Both during the preparations for the March, then during the converging of the Marchers on Corstorphine, and finally over the historic three days and the return, the *Daily Worker* featured the March. We believe, however, the Holyrood Palace incident itself is sufficient commentary on the value of the workers' own Press.

PRINCES STREET

That night another desperate attempt was made to disorganise and disperse the March. Accommodation was again refused; no hall, nothing could be found; if the Marchers cared, the Meadows were available to them.

But it didn't demoralise these Marchers. After an indignant, gigantic Protest Meeting at the Mound, another deputation returned from meeting the Authorities. "Only the streets are left to us", they reported. A roar from the Marchers and the workers of Edinburgh - "All right, we'll sleep in the street; but by God, we'll pick the streets to sleep in!"

Form up! Off to - where? Direct to Princes Street directly below the flood-lit Edinburgh Castle, directly opposite the plutocratic Conservative and Liberal Clubs and the palatial hotels! The whistle goes, "Packs off! Make yourselves comfortable, boys; here's your bed for the night!"

Never in all its history has Edinburgh witnessed anything like what followed. Right along the South pavement in the most aristocratic street in Britain lay the Hunger Marchers - blankets and newspapers spread out for mattresses! The wealthy dress-suited plutocracy as they came from their clubs and banquets, goggled, absolutely goggled! Here are excerpts from the Edinburgh Press, which showed their amazement:

PRESS REPORTS

"At a fairly late hour there was no sign of them dispersing, but it was a surprise to the large number of citizens remaining on Princes Street to see them spread out along the south pavement, set down their equipment, and prepare to stay there.

The spectacle was amazing. Behind the huddled marchers was the Castle, brilliantly flood-lit, while on the north pavement strong forces of police patrolled and kept the crowds of bewildered theatre-goers and others on the move. Motorists stopped to survey the extraordinary scene before they were moved on, and practically all traffic - quite considerable for a time - had to use the north side of the street to avoid the equipment of the marchers.

This surprising manoeuvre suffered no interference from the police. The marchers were orderly, though several high-spirited sections were occasionally noisy.

WALKING UNTIL DAWN

"With banners stacked against the railings of the gardens and the last tunes played on the flute bands, some of the marchers equipped with proper sleeping bags turned in for the night, with shoes, etc, set on the kerb. Others paraded up and down amongst the sleeping forms, but after a couple of hours nearly everyone was either asleep or dozing.

The first hour or so was passed in proper camp-fire manner with, occasionally, songs and choruses, whilst remarks such as 'Let's put out the lights and go to sleep', greeted the extinguishing of the Castle flood-lighting system. It was indeed the 'Lights Out', however, and the camp became quiet, patrolled at the distance of the width of the street by the police." - *Edinburgh Dispatch*

"Historic Princes Street has known many unusual sights, but that presented this morning when the marchers' camp, extending for over two hundred yards, from midway between Hanover and Frederick Streets to midway between Castle Street, was unique.

It had to be seen to be believed. Men and women were rising from their hard couches while citizens were passing to their work by motor car, tram and on foot.

Men shaved with their mirrors supported on the railings of West Princes Street Gardens, which were kept closed, and others washed and dried themselves at a fountain in the middle of the marchers' encampment. Policemen in twos and threes marched up and down.

One man slept in a bathing suit, with a newspaper as a mattress and a single blanket as cover. Another rose this morning and wrote a song,

'For Liberty', which he proudly showed to his leaders.

It is impossible for passers-by to walk along the area of footpath occupied by the marchers. Walking along on the carriageway one heard snatches of conversation:-

'Slept well?'

'How did ye enjoy yer feather bed?'

'Did ye feel a draught coming in during the night?'

A WOMAN DRUMMER

They were a good-natured crowd, laughing and joking. An early morning urn of steaming tea was brought to them, and they proceeded to entertain themselves - and passers-by - until their breakfast arrived. They sang, flutes were played, while a women put on the big drum and started banging it while another clashed cymbals; there was an attempt at dancing, and a youth showed how a drum-major's staff should be swung. Right at the western end of the camp, Mr McGovern MP, one of the leaders, lay 'abed' cleaning his shoes, when an *Evening Dispatch* representative made a tour of the marchers this morning. By his side, Mr McShane, another of the leaders, lay stretched out." - *Edinburgh Dispatch*

THE MARCHERS' STRENGTH

Were they demoralised? Did the Authorities' plan succeed of intimidating and frightening the Marchers by forcing them to sleep out on the pavements? No!

It was the Authorities who were demoralised and panicky. The Marchers - men and women - inspired by their cause, feeling and knowing they had the support of the working masses everywhere, were more determined, more united, more militant than ever. Their spirit of self-imposed discipline had been tested and emerged with flying colours.

So determined were the men that they beat the police objections to having their meals in Princes Street and had their breakfast and dinner there. Princes Street - which had been turned into a dormitory by the actions of the Authorities - was now turned into an open-air dining place by the Marchers themselves!

By this time the Press, that tried to ignore the March, was pestering us for interviews. The following from the Edinburgh *Evening News* of 13th June is an example, and explains to some extent the situation on the morning after sleeping on the street:

"Mr John McGovern and Mr McShane were among the first to rise from their open-air 'bunks', and by eight o'clock most of the men were recovering some of the spiritedness which they have displayed, and were sitting against the railings, laughing and jesting, while supplies of food were rushed from the field-Kitchens at Simon Square and tea was being served steaming hot from large and well-filled dixie cans. A number were still too much overcome by fatigue to bother about food.

'THE GREATEST STREET! LOOK AT IT NOW!'

Mr Harry McShane and Mr Aitken Ferguson, another member of the Council in charge of the marchers, in conversation with an *Evening News* representative in Princes Street this morning, said they regarded the action of the authorities in not giving them accommodation last night as a trumpery evasion, and they thought it was clear that the authorities were making efforts to drive them out of the city. They were determined that they would not be driven out in that way, and even if they had to 'grow into the ground' they would continue to make their sleeping quarters in Princes Street. The previous night, the police had obtained them accommodation within ten minutes. Now the authorities were prepared to allow nearly 1,000 men and women to remain exposed to the elements of a night in the open without regard to health.
'Here is the greatest street in Europe', added Mr Ferguson; 'just look at it now!'
Mr McShane said he had taken part in five Hunger Marches altogether, and in not one city had he had such an experience as to have been compelled to remain in the streets all night.
Mr Ferguson cynically recalled that a week or two ago Mr McGovern had been invited to attend the General Assembly in Edinburgh as the guest of Mr John Buchan. Mr McGovern had now visited Edinburgh, and was given the hospitality of Princes Street along with the marchers, instead of Holyrood Palace.

'HERE WE ARE AND HERE WE STAY'

'In view of this new situation', added Mr McShane, 'Mr McGovern had been contemplating remaining in Edinburgh instead of attending the House of Commons for the unemployment debate tomorrow. The Marchers' Council had been considering the matter, and were of the opinion that Mr McGovern should go to London to bring attention to the plight of the marchers from a national platform.

'So far', said Mr McShane, 'here we are and here we stay until another decision is reached. We can breakfast, dinner or tea here, and the men require a rest. They can have that rest in Princes Street. We have decided to give them a long lie in "bed" this morning' - *Edinburgh Evening News*

THE TOWN CLERK WANTS A GUARANTEE

It was clear that the March had stirred Edinburgh to its very depths. Nothing like it had ever occurred to disturb the repose of Scotland's Capital. The job was now to mobilise Scotland to organise the sympathy and support which existed to carry on a fight in every county, town and village for the development of schemes of work and relief scales.

A deputation on behalf of the Marchers, consisting of the Rev. Mr Marwick and Capt. JR White*, interviewed the Authorities on the question of accommodation for the Marchers, but without success.

Then it was decided that the March should approach the PAC on this and other questions. A very heated discussion ensued between the Marchers' deputation and the PAC officer in Edinburgh, Mr Douglas, a most impudent and self-satisfied individual, who informed the deputation that the PAC was open day and night for applications.

On the return of the deputation, they were informed that the Assistant Chief Constable and the Town Clerk Depute had proposals to make to the March leadership. These proposals were: -

(1) That the Authorities were prepared to pay the Balance (over £30) towards the cost of Transport of the Marchers returning to their homes;

(2) That this would only be done provided that a guarantee was given that no more Marches to Edinburgh would take place.

They were told promptly and straightly that there would be no such guarantee given.

---

*Capt JR White was an Irish Protestant, republican and socialist. He organised the Irish Citizen Army to defend strikers from attack in the 1913 Dublin lockout. This body later formed the nucleus of Connolly's Citizen Army. White fought with the Irish Republican Brigade in the Spanish Civil War, became increasingly dismayed by the manipulation of the International Brigades by the Communists and resigned his command and worked for the anarcho-syndicalist CNT.

THE PAC BLUFF CALLED

Immediately they left, the marchers formed up and set off to the PAC Office. The March was calling the bluff of Mr Douglas and the PAC. Six hundred Marchers, supported by Edinburgh workers, lined up in order to make the individual application for accommodation which Mr Douglas had boasted of being ready to receive - and the result? Complete and total collapse of the Edinburgh PAC.

A tremendous outburst of anger from the Marchers at the refusal of the PAC to do anything preceded a huge mass demonstration of Edinburgh workers who came to join the Marchers. Back to Princes Street, and then at 11pm, a terrific demonstration through the City.

Edinburgh was out to a man - roused, militant. The courage and determination of the Marchers had lit a flame of struggle among the masses of the Edinburgh workers.

Never was there such a turnout and such enthusiasm. The Marchers and workers were one, fused in a common struggle against the capitalist governors.

It was a staggering blow to the authorities - a victory thenceforth was assured. Halls were speedily secured by the workers and the Marchers were housed that night.

THE FINAL DAY

The next day was the question of driving home the advantages gained. The following report from the *Edinburgh Evening News* of 14th June explains fairly well the situation on the Wednesday morning.

"Mr McGovern MP and Mr McShane proceeded to the City Chambers in the forenoon for the purpose of making representations with regard to the position of the marchers in the city.

There was being held at the time a meeting of the Lord Provost's Committee of the Town Council, which had been specially called to consider the situation. The meeting was private, and at the close the Press representatives were informed that no statement would be made regarding the proceedings.

Mr McGovern and Mr McShane were not received by the Committee, but after the meeting, consultations took place between them and Mr Mackinnon, the Depute Chief Constable.

They left the building evidently dissatisfied with the result of their mission. Their demands were for food and accommodation for the men, or, alternatively, for free transport for the marchers to their homes.

THANKS TO THE CITIZENS

Mr Aitken Ferguson, on behalf of the Marchers' Council, stated that he would like to convey his appreciation of the response which the citizens of Edinburgh had given to the appeal of the marchers, and he mentioned that plans were being considered for a much bigger march to Edinburgh in the near future.

Chalked on the causeway in Simon Square, in bold letters, was the message: 'Edinburgh Workers Solidarity Wins Scottish Hunger Marchers a Bed' - obviously an appreciation of the local efforts made for the comfort of the marchers last night." - *Edinburgh Evening News*

It should be mentioned, however, that when negotiations broke down, the deputation gave the Authorities an hour to provide a meal, failing which - in view of the fact that the Public Assistance Committee had refused to accept applications for relief - we would take other steps to secure a meal. This had the effect of having the Authorities telling us to spend the £30 we had earmarked for the buses. When we said - What about the buses, then? we were told confidentially that the buses would be all right. Later a meeting of Marchers was held at which a report was given. An effigy of Sir Godfrey Collins was burnt. A further meal was provided, while a deputation went to the Ministry of Labour to raise the question of paying benefit to the Marchers for days they were on the march. No progress was made here.

About 5.30 the buses arrived for the Marchers, without any guarantee being given and without any payment being made by the Marchers. The working class had broken through! A smashing victory had been obtained! At the last meeting of the Marchers in Edinburgh, when the final report was given, telegrams of support came from all quarters - Notts and Derby, Teeside, London, Glasgow. A telegram from Calton announcing reinforcements ready to leave drew a storm of cheers.

Where was the guarantee of no future Hunger March? Dropped like a hot brick in the face of the Marchers' refusal and the solidarity of the workers!

THE MARCHERS COME HOME

And the welcome given to the returning Marchers! In Glasgow, for example, the streets were black with people waiting for the buses; meetings lasting until well after midnight were held in the presence of tremendous, cheering crowds. The very mention of Unity and the United Front invariably drew tumultuous cheers.

Edinburgh capitalists hope they have seen the last of the Hunger Marchers. Their hopes are in vain and doomed to disappointment.

OUR LESSONS

The March has shown the tremendous militancy and feeling for Unity which exists all over Scotland. It has demonstrated clearly before the eyes of all, that while the masses of the workers are steadily coming together, the leadership and the policy of the Labour Party and Trade Unions in the main supports Capitalism.

Profiles

John McGovern, Aitken Ferguson, Harry McShane

John McGovern MP was a controversial figure to say the least. Even his adoption as the Labour candidate for the Shettleston constituency on the death of John Wheatley was not without controversy, and he was expelled from the Labour Party, for allegedly using trade union delegates with forged credentials to vote for his nomination. He then joined the Independent Labour Party (ILP). In some ways he was quite militant. As well as being arrested with Harry McShane over the issue, he also refused to leave the House of Commons after demanding that the House discuss the jailing of the Tramp Preachers, jailed for speaking on Glasgow Green without the Town Council's consent - and was forcibly removed from the House and suspended for six months. On the following Sunday he spoke on the Green on the Free Speech Platform with Guy Aldred* and Harry McShane. He always supported the Hunger Marchers, though he hated the Communist Party.

After having been associated with the ILP, the Labour Party and the Anarchist Federation he started to defend the Royalty, and eventually became an ardent speaker for the extreme right wing Moral Re-armament Movement. His last political act after he stood down as a Labour candidate was to recommend a vote for the Conservatives in the 1964 general election.

Aitken Ferguson, who played a prominent role in the Edinburgh Hunger March had been in the working class movement for many years, and at one time he was the secretary of the Socialist Labour Party. He was probably one of the best read persons in the movement, and after he joined the Communist Party he always played a leading role in working class activity. In fact he was the only member of the Communist Party, apart from Harry McShane, who spoke on the Free Speech Platform during the campaign against the ban on free speech on the Glasgow Green. He was at one time a secretary in the Western Bureau of the Communist International in Germany, and worked with George Dimitroff.†

Ferguson always had a strong belief in Scottish independence, and during the attempt to form the Scottish Convention in 1938 he was put into the

---

*An anarchist and a Marxist, in 1921 Aldred helped to set up the Anti-Parliamentary Communist Federation in opposition to the parliamentarism of the newly formed Communist Party.
†Secretary of the Communist International.

office to help organise it, but the outbreak of war ended the whole idea, though he did write extensively on the Scottish struggle and had a few pamphlets published. During the war he joined the Anglo-Russian Oil Company as a director and remained there until his death.

Harry McShane was one of the first socialists of the 1920's to realise the importance of organising the unemployed, and apart from John MacLean* was regarded as the spokesman for the unemployed in Scotland. In 1922 he made the first attempt at organisation with a meeting, in a cafe in Glasgow's Argyle Street, of representatives from the Vale of Leven and Lanarkshire. He contacted Wal Hannington, the NUWM National Organiser in London, and a Scottish contingent was organised to participate in the first national hunger march to London in October/November 1922, though he couldn't join it as he was on bail. While it was widely recognised that the Communist Party had a large influence in the NUWM, McShane rejected their proposals on many occasions, insisting that all policy decisions be taken by the marchers.

McShane was a very well read man, and a great admirer of Adam Ferguson, the 18th century Scottish philosopher. Unlike many leading Communists he welcomed dialogue and was an excellent debater, but more than anything he liked to be involved in struggle - whether it be strikes, demonstrations or protests over housing, he was in his element. McShane left the Communist Party in 1953, because of the Party's increasing Stalinism and reformism, its lack of internal democracy, and its attempts to make him toe the party line. At the age of sixty two he went back to his trade as an engineer, but continued to speak in the open air on street corners. He became the president of his trade union branch and a delegate to Glasgow Trades Council. One of the last meetings he spoke at was in 1987 on the Mayday platform on Glasgow Green at a remembrance of the bi-centenary of the Calton Weaver Martyrs†. He was aged ninety six when he died in Baxter House, an old folks home in Glasgow in 1988. A few days before he died, when asked how he was fixed for money, his reply was "fine, I have got over forty pounds, you know". After eighty years a Marxist, let that be his epitaph.

Hugh Savage

---

*Scotland's best known Marxist, MacLean was imprisoned in 1918 for inciting sedition and mutiny. He never joined the Communist Party, and in 1923 he founded the Scottish Workers' Republican Party.
†During Glasgow's first recorded industrial strike, six striking weavers were killed by soldiers on 3rd September 1787.

Acknowledgements

Les Foster resigned from the Communist Party in 1953 with Hugh Savage and Harry McShane. He was active in the squatters movement and led the famous squat in the Grand Hotel in Glasgow. A builder's labourer and shop steward in the Glasgow Corporation, he was at the forefront of the successful strike action to prevent the sale of council houses at Merrylee in 1951. From 1955 he worked as a railman until his retirement. Les is the author (with Hugh Savage) of a biography of Willie Nairn - *All for the Cause* and (with Ned Donaldson) of *Sell and be Damned* - the story of the Merrylee housing scandal.

Hugh Savage left the Communist Party in 1953. He was a plumber to trade, a well-known shipyard shop steward and an executive member of Glasgow Trades Council. He was active on housing issues in Glasgow. In recent years he has been prominent in the fight to save Glasgow Green from private development and the campaign in defence of Elspeth King and Michael Donnelly, former curators of the Peoples' Palace. At present Hugh is Chairman of the Friends of the Peoples' Palace. He is the author (with Les Foster) of *All for the Cause*.

UNEMPLOYED ORGANISE

Join the N.U.W.M.

The N.U.W.M. was established in 1920. It has been the organiser and leader of all the struggles of the Unemployed for improved conditions since that time.

It has proved times out of number that by activity and organisation, the Central and Local Government authorities can be compelled to make concessions for improvements in the conditions of the Unemployed.

The N.U.W.M. is fighting for :—

1. Abolition of the Means Test.
2. Abolition of the Anomalies Regulations.
3. Abolition of Task Work.
4. For Work Schemes at T.U. Rates.
5. Restoration of the benefit cuts.
6. Increased scales of Relief.
7. And many other improvements in the interest of the unemployed.

In addition to carrying out constant mass activity the Movement can protect your Unemployment Benefit claims at Labour Exchange, Court of Referees and Umpire. During the year 1932 the Legal Department of the N.U.W.M. fought 1,529 Unemployment Insurance Appeals of members before the Umpire and recovered £5,000 in benefits

---

Headquarters Address:
11a White Lion Street, London, E.1.

Published by the N.U.W.M., 183 George Street, Glasgow and printed by Kirkwood & Co., 127 Stockwell Street, Glasgow, C.1

SOME RECENT TITLES FROM AK PRESS

SOME RECENT ATTACKS: ESSAYS CULTURAL AND POLITICAL - by James Kelman
ISBN 1 873176 80 5; 96pp; £4.50.
In this collection, Kelman directs his linguistic craftsmanship and scathing humour at targets ranging from "private profit and public loss" to the "endemic racism, class bias and general elitism at the English end of the Anglo-American literary tradition."

POLL TAX REBELLION - by Danny Burns
ISBN 1 873176 50 3 208pp; £4.95.
Using a combination of text, photos and graphics, and drawing on the voices of activists and non-payers *Poll Tax Rebellion* describes the everyday organisation of local anti-poll tax groups, and chronicles the demonstrations and riots leading up to the battle of Trafalgar - showing how the Poll Tax was destroyed.

UNFINISHED BUSINESS: THE POLITICS OF CLASS WAR.
ISBN 1 873176 45 7 192pp; £4.50.
Class War's comprehensive statement of political intent and action. Chapters on capitalism, the state, class, class struggle, revolution, organisation and a new world, discuss the present situation, how we arrived here, and a way forward. "Despite the politicians of the right and left trying to wish us out of existence, our class, the working class, are still here: alive and kicking!"

SABOTAGE IN THE AMERICAN WORKPLACE: ANECDOTES OF DISSATISFACTION, MISCHIEF AND REVENGE - by Martin Sprouse
ISBN 1 873176 65 1; 184pp; £9.95.
A sensational collection of first hand accounts of workplace sabotage - from theft to computer logic bombs to armed robbery. Anyone who has dreaded another day at work should read it.

AK PRESS PUBLISHES, DISTRIBUTES TO THE TRADE AND RETAILS MAIL ORDER A WIDE VARIETY OF RADICAL LITERATURE. FOR OUR LATEST CATALOGUE FEATURING THESE AND SEVERAL THOUSAND OTHER TITLES, PLEASE SEND A LARGE SELF-ADDRESSED, STAMPED ENVELOPE TO:

AK Press
22 Lutton Place
Edinburgh, Scotland
EH8 9PE, Great Britain

AK Press
P.O. Box 40682
San Francisco, CA
94140-0682 U.S.A.